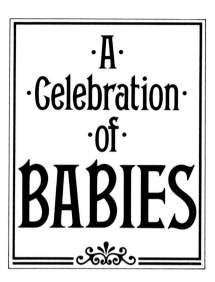

·A·
·Celebration·
·of·
BABIES

D1637809

Beneath an Angel's Wing
WILLIAM STRUTT
1825-1915

·A· ·Celebration· ·of· BABIES

An anthology
of poetry and prose
edited by

Sally Emerson

Blackie

To Anna

British Library Cataloguing in Publication Data
A Celebration of babies.
   1. Parenthood – Literary collections   2. English
   literature
   I. Emerson, Sally
   820.8'03520431   PR1111.P3

   ISBN 0-216-91864-2
   ISBN 0-216-92776-5 Pbk

Blackie and Son Limited
7 Leicester Place, London WC2H 7BP

Designed by Malcolm Smythe

Studio Del & Co.

Typeset in Sabon by
Rowland Phototypesetting (London) Ltd

Printed in Great Britain by
Cambus Litho, East Kilbride

Woodcuts throughout the book are by Arthur Hughes,
from *Sing Song* by Christina Rossetti.
'The Mother' on page 61 is by J Lavery ARA. The photographs
on pages 25 and 48 are reproduced by permission of The Mansell
Collection. All the other photographs are antique postcards
from Sally Emerson's own collection.

Contents

INTRODUCTION

Only one person gave me any idea of what having a baby would be like. She said the nearest thing to it was a passionate love affair. I thought she was being silly.

Others had told me, more realistically I thought, of endless nappies, broken nights, runny noses, continual tiredness. I was therefore somewhat dreading the arrival of the baby, whom I was determined not to let disrupt my well-ordered existence.

But as I lay in my hospital bed the day after the birth, everything seemed quite different, and has been ever since. My past life struck me as interesting but rather tawdry, like a bad movie full of stagey love scenes and brittle, competitive people. The reality was here, lying asleep in her cot, knowing yet innocent, like some ancient guru who had been here since the world began and yet had only just arrived.

I loved her with a love more intense than any I had known before, and when I returned home I searched for writing which expressed this particular brand of love. There were endless anthologies of love poems about men and women but not one about babies.

Over the months, as she grew and developed and continued to delight and enthrall me with her beauty, her spirited innocence, her gaiety and her sense of humour, I continued to find here and there, often in the oddest places, in Dickens, in the ancient Greek writer Sappho, in the poems of the dissolute Swinburne, words which caught something of the extraordinary interest of babies.

I decided to create my own anthology, the book I should like to give to friends who have just had babies. For, as Antonia Byatt writes, "She thought she would never forget any of these moments, these points of development, these markers in time, and forgot all of them as the next stage seemed to be ... eternal." This celebration captures and holds such moments.

The men, from Dickens to Laurie Lee, have many of the best lines, perhaps because women throughout the ages have been too enraptured by their new charges, or too exhausted by them, to sit back and record their wonderment. Or maybe they are not as surprised by their pride and delight as men like William Cox Bennett, who wrote of his daughter:

> Loveliness beyond completeness,
> Sweetness distancing all sweetness,
> Beauty all that beauty may be –
> That's May Bennett, that's my baby.

Perhaps it is only the new generation of liberated women, unaccustomed to babies, nervous of babies, often dreading babies, who will encounter the joy of motherhood with that particular shock which gives rise to literature.

SALLY EMERSON

BIRTH

Oh, fields of wonder
Out of which
Stars are born,
And moon and sun
And me as well,
Like stroke
Of lightning
In the night
Some mark
To make
Some word
To tell.

LANGSTON HUGHES

This then was my daughter, born in the autumn and a late fall into my life, lying purple and dented like a little bruised plum, as though she'd been lightly trodden in the grass and forgotten.

Then the Matron picked her up and she came suddenly alive, her bent legs kicking crabwise, and the first living gesture I saw was a thin wringing of the hands accompanied by a far-out Hebridean lament.

This moment of meeting seemed to be a birthtime for both of us; her first and my second life. Nothing, I knew, could ever be the same again, and I think I was reasonably shaken. I peered intently at her, looking for familiar signs, but she was as convulsed as an Aztec idol. Was this really my daughter, this purple concentration of grief, this blind and protesting dwarf?

Then they handed her to me, stiff and howling, and I held her for the first time and kissed her, and she went still and quiet as though by instinctive guile, and I was instantly enslaved by her flattery of my powers.

Newborn, of course, she looked already a centenarian, tottering on the brink of an old crone's grave, exhausted, shrunken, bald as Voltaire, mopping, mowing, and twisting wrinkled claws in speechless spasms of querulous doom.

But with each day of survival, once her mother had brought her home, she grew younger and fatter, her face drawing on life, every breath of real air healing the birth-death stain she had worn so witheringly at the beginning.

This girl then, my child, this parcel of will and warmth, began to fill the cottage with her obsessive purpose. The rhythmic tides of her sleeping and feeding spaciously measured our days and nights. Her frail absorption was a commanding presence, her helplessness strong as a rock, so that I found myself listening even to her silences as though some great engine was purring upstairs . . . .

She was of course just an ordinary miracle, but was also the particular late wonder of my life. So almost every night, at first, I'd take her to bed like a book and lie close and study her. Her dark blue eyes would stare straight into mine, but off-centre, not seeing me.

Such moments could have been the best we would ever know, those midnights of mutual blindness, while I was safe from her first recognitions, and she'd stare idly through me, at the pillow, at the bedhead, at the light on the wall, and each was a shadow of indifferent importance.

Here she was then, my daughter, here, alive, the one I must possess and guard. A year before this space had been empty, not even a hope of her was in it. Now she was here, brand new, with our name upon her, and no one could call in the night to reclaim her.

LAURIE LEE,
from *Two Women*

LOVE ME

Love me, – I love you,
    Love me, my baby;
Sing it high, sing it low,
    Sing it as may be.

Mother's arms under you,
    Her eyes above you
Sing it high, sing it low,
    Love me, – I love you.

CHRISTINA ROSSETTI

Morning Song

Love set you going like a fat gold watch,
The midwife slapped your footsoles, and your bald cry
Took its place among the elements.

Our voices echo, magnifying your arrival. New statue.
In a drafty museum, your nakedness
Shadows our safety. We stand round blankly as walls.

I'm no more your mother
Than the cloud that distils a mirror to reflect its own slow
Effacement at the wind's hand.

All night your moth-breath
Flickers among the flat pink roses. I wake to listen:
A far sea moves in my ear.

One cry, and I stumble from bed, cow-heavy and floral
In my Victorian nightgown.
Your mouth opens clean as a cat's. The window square

Whitens and swallows its dull stars. And now you try
Your handful of notes;
The clear vowels rise like balloons.

SYLVIA PLATH

NEVER AGAIN AN EASY HOUR

Monday 9th October 1775

My wife having been seized with her pains in the night, I got up about three o'clock, and between four and five Dr Young came. He and I sat upstairs mostly till between three and four, when, after we had dined, her labour became violent. I was full of expectation, and meditated curiously on the thought that it was already certain of what sex the child was, but that I could not have the least guess on which side the probability was.... I did not feel so much anxiety about my wife now as on former occasions, being better used to an inlying. Yet the danger was as great now as ever. I was easier from the same deception which affects a soldier who has escaped in several battles. She was very ill. Between seven and eight I went into the room. She was just delivered. I heard her say, 'God be thanked for whatever he sends.' I supposed then the child was a daughter. But she herself had not then seen it. Miss Preston said, 'Is it a daughter?' 'No,' said Mrs Forrest, the nurse-keeper, 'it's a son.' When I had seen the little man I said that I should now be so anxious that probably I should never again have an easy hour. I said to Dr Young with great seriousness, 'Doctor, Doctor, let no man set his heart upon anything in this world but land or heritable bonds; for he has no security that anything else will last as long as himself.' My anxiety subdued a flutter of joy which was in my breast. I wrote several letters to announce my son's birth. I indulged some imaginations that he might perhaps be a great man.

JAMES BOSWELL,
from his *Diary*

THE BIRTHNIGHT: TO F.
(The poet's daughter, Florence)

Dearest, it was a night
That in its darkness rocked Orion's stars;
A sighing wind ran faintly white
Along the willows, and the cedar boughs
Laid their wide hands in stealthy peace across
The starry silence of their antique moss:
No sound save rushing air
Cold, yet all sweet with Spring,
And in thy mother's arms, crouched weeping there,
        Thou, lovely thing.

WALTER DE LA MARE

15

MIGHTY LIKE A ROSE

Sweetest little feller,
Everybody knows;
Don't know what to call him,
But he's mighty like a rose.

Looking at his Mammy
With eyes so shiny blue,
Make you think that heaven
Is coming close to you.

FRANK L. STANTON

OYSTERS AND CHAMPAGNE

The character of a child is already plain, even in its mother's womb. Before I was born my mother was in great agony of spirit and in a tragic situation. She could take no food except iced oysters and champagne. If people ask me when I began to dance I reply, 'In my mother's womb, probably as a result of the oysters and champagne – the food of Aphrodite'.

ISADORA DUNCAN,
My Life, 1927

SHEER PLEASURE

Being pregnant was horrible. I worried myself ill about eating and drinking the wrong things, and fainted in telephone kiosks. I didn't feel much sense of communion with the unborn, though I know others do. Labour wasn't much fun either, until the last stages. But the last stages were spectacular. Ah, what an incomparable thrill. All that heaving, the amazing damp slippery wetness and hotness, the confused sight of dark grey ropes of cord, the blood, the baby's cry. The sheer pleasure of the feeling of a born baby on one's thighs is like nothing on earth.

MARGARET DRABBLE
'With All My Love, (Signed) Mama'

BEING BORN IS IMPORTANT

Being born is important.
You who have stood at the bedposts
and seen a mother on her high harvest day,
the day of the most golden of harvest moons for her.

You who have seen the new wet child
dried behind the ears,
swaddled in soft fresh garments,
pursing its lips and sending a groping mouth
toward the nipples where white milk is ready –

You who have seen this love's payday
of wild toil and sweet agonizing –

You know being born is important.
You know nothing else was ever so important to you.
You understand the payday of love is so old,
So involved, so traced with circles of the moon,
So cunning with the secrets of the salts of the blood –
It must be older than the moon, older than salt.

CARL SANDBURG

The Firstborn (detail)
FRED W. ELWELL
1870-1958

A Scottish Christening (detail)
JOHN PHILLIP
1817-1867

Choosing a Name

I have got a new-born sister;
I was nigh the first that kissed her.
When the nursing woman brought her
To papa, his infant daughter,
How papa's dear eye did glisten!
She will shortly be to christen:
And papa has made the offer,
I shall have the naming of her.

Now I wonder what would please her,
Charlotte, Julia, or Louisa.
Ann and Mary, they're too common;
Joan's too formal for a woman;
Jane's a prettier name beside;
But we had a Jane that died.
They would say, if 'twas Rebecca,
That she was a little Quaker.
Edith's pretty, but that looks
Better in old English books;
Ellen's left off long ago;
Blanche is out of fashion now.
None that I have named as yet
Are so good as Margaret.
Emily is neat and fine.
What do you think of Caroline?
How I'm puzzled and perplexed
What to choose or think of next!
I am in a little fever.
Lest the name that I shall give her
Should disgrace her or defame her,
I will leave papa to name her.

CHARLES AND MARY LAMB

BOGART AND SON

We'd taken our usual trip to New York and celebrated our third anniversary. I remember saying we'd never had a honeymoon, to which Bogie rightly retorted, 'You've been on a three-year honeymoon – ever since we've been married.' Then I missed a period. I rushed to the calendar, marked it, and prayed. I counted every day until I missed the second. I'd had a false alarm once before.

I called Red Krohn and went in for my rabbit test. He called me: 'Yes, ma'am, you are pregnant.' I rushed to see him, he examined me and said absolutely – it would be around the end of December. The joy – the joy! I'd have to set the stage for Bogie's homecoming that evening – he'd faint when he heard. He didn't faint. I don't know what happened, but after I told him, we had the biggest fight we'd ever had. I was in tears – this moment I'd been hoping for, waiting for, was a disaster. I should have learned right then never to act out a scene before it's played. Bogie was full of sound and fury signifying that he hadn't married me to lose me to a child – no child was going to come between us. The next morning he wrote me a long letter apologizing for his behaviour, saying he didn't know what had gotten into him except his fear of losing me – a child was an unknown quantity to him. He didn't know what kind of father he'd make. He was so afraid our closeness and incredible happiness together would be cut into by a child – but of course he wanted us to have a baby more than anything in the world, he just would have to get used to the idea. He'd spent forty-eight years childless, and had never really considered that being a father would ever become a reality at this point in his life....

Two days before I was to bring my baby home, Los Angeles had its first snowfall in fifty years. I remember sitting in my hospital bed and looking out the window – I thought I was imagining things. What a great dividend – only right for the child of Eastern-born parents! I couldn't wait to get home. I could have a baby every nine months if it was this easy! I hoped Bogie was as happy as I was. As for me, I knew that I had it all – and Bogie had given it to me.

On January 11 the ambulance took Steve and me home. As we were carried to the front door, there on the lawn was an enormous snowman which Bogie had spent half the night building. It was odd to see snow covering camellia bushes. I was taken to our bedroom, Steve to his at the other end of the house. We had an intercom rigged so that I could hear every sound in the nursery – could talk to the nurse if I wished. It was kept on at all times....

My first morning home I was having breakfast in bed when Bogie went off to work. Before he left, he stopped in to see his son – I had the intercom on and suddenly heard in a soft, new voice, 'Hello, son. You're a little fella, aren't you? I'm Father. Welcome home.'

LAUREN BACALL,
from *By Myself*

I Had Expected So Little

The midwife asked me if I would like to see the child. 'Please,' I said gratefully, and she went away and came back with my daughter wrapped up in a small grey bloodstained blanket, and with a ticket saying Stacey round her ankle. She put her in my arms and I sat there looking at her, and her great wide blue eyes looked at me with seeming recognition, and what I felt it is pointless to try to describe. Love, I suppose one might call it, and the first of my life.

I had expected so little, really. I never expect much. I had been told of the ugliness of newborn children, of their red and wrinkled faces, their waxy covering, their emaciated limbs, their hairy cheeks, their piercing cries. All I can say is that mine was beautiful and in my defence I must add that others said she was beautiful too. She was not red nor even wrinkled, but palely soft, each feature delicately reposed in its right place, and she was not bald but adorned with a thick, startling crop of black hair. One of the nurses fetched a brush and flattened it down and it covered her forehead, lying in a dense fringe that reached to her eyes. And her eyes, that seemed to see me and that looked into mine with deep gravity and charm, were a profound blue, the whites white with the gleam of alarming health. When they asked if they could have her back and put her back in her cradle for the night, I handed her over without reluctance, for the delight of holding her was too much for me. I felt as well as they that such pleasure should be regulated and rationed.

MARGARET DRABBLE,
from *The Millstone*

SONG

Where did you come from, baby dear?
Out of everywhere into here.

Where did you get your eyes so blue?
Out of the sky as I came through.

Where did you get that little tear?
I found it waiting when I got here.

What makes your forehead so smooth and high?
A soft hand stroked it as I went by.

What makes your cheek like a warm white rose?
I saw something better than anyone knows.

GEORGE MacDONALD

Dombey and Son

Dombey sat in the corner of the darkened room in the great armchair by the bedside, and Son lay tucked up warm in a little basket bedstead, carefully disposed on a low settee immediately in front of the fire and close to it, as if his constitution were analogous to that of a muffin, and it was essential to toast him brown while he was very new.

Dombey was about eight-and-forty years of age. Son about eight-and-forty minutes. Dombey was rather bald, rather red, and though a handsome well-made man, too stern and pompous in appearance to be prepossessing. Son was very bald, and very red, and though (of course) an undeniably fine infant, somewhat crushed and spotty in his general effect, as yet. On the brow of Dombey, Time and his brother Care had set some marks, as on a tree that was to come down in good time – remorseless twins they are for striding through their human forests, notching as they go – while the countenance of Son was crossed with a thousand little creases, which the same deceitful Time would take delight in smoothing out and wearing away with the flat part of his scythe, as a preparation of the surface for his deeper operations.

Dombey, exulting in the long-looked-for event, jingled and jingled the heavy gold watch-chain that depended from below his trim blue coat, whereof the buttons sparkled phosphorescently in the feeble rays of the distant fire. Son, with his little fists curled up and clenched, seemed, in his feeble way, to be squaring at existence for having come upon him so unexpectedly.

CHARLES DICKENS,
from *Dombey and Son*

Born Yesterday
for Sally Amis

Tightly-folded bud,
I have wished you something
None of the others would:
Not the usual stuff
About being beautiful,
Or running off a spring
Of innocence and love –
They will all wish you that,
And should it prove possible,
Well, you're a lucky girl.

But if it shouldn't, then
May you be ordinary;
Have, like other women,
An average of talents:
Not ugly, not good-looking,
Nothing uncustomary
To pull you off your balance,
That, unworkable itself,
Stops all the rest from working.
In fact, may you be dull –
If that is what a skilled,
Vigilant, flexible,
Unemphasized, enthralled
Catching of happiness is called.

PHILIP LARKIN

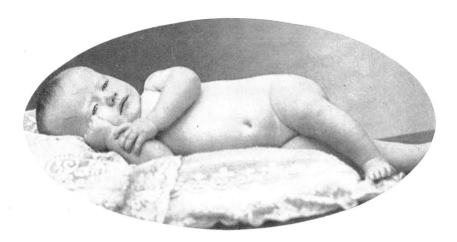

When the nurse took my first child and put him to my breast his tiny mouth opened and reached for me as if he had known forever what to do. He began to suck with such force it took my breath away. It was like being attached to a vacuum cleaner. I began to laugh. I couldn't help myself. It seemed incredible that such a tiny creature could have such force and determination. He too had a purpose. He was raw, insistent and real. With every fibre of his being, this child was drawing his life. And he would not be denied.

Tears of joy ran shamelessly down my cheeks while he sucked. I thought back to my past conviction that only when I had a baby would *I know* whatever it was I had to know. Now I *did* know. It is the only important thing I have ever learned, and so ridiculously simple: love exists. It's real and honest and unbelievably solid in a world where far too much is complex or confusing or false.

There, in the midst of all that clinical green and white, I had discovered what love was all about. It was a meeting of two beings. The age, the sex, the relationship didn't matter. That day, two creatures – he and I – had met. We touched each other, in utter honesty and simplicity. There was nothing romantic or solemn about it. No obligations, no duties, no fancy games. We'd met. Just that. Somewhere in spirit we were friends. I knew beyond all doubt that I'd found something *real*. And real it has remained.

Now my eldest child is almost nineteen and it is a long time since that first day when I held him, not knowing what I should do next. Somehow we would find what to do and what to say to one another. It was only a question of being still enough to listen to each other, and having faith. That faith has never left me. Love exists... real love... not the kind that depends on who you are or how you look or whether or not you are kind to someone. This meeting – this sharing – this naked confrontation where two beings are, for an instant, together. Now I could live with all the fancy adult games and be indifferent to them. I would always be able to bear the feeling of emptiness that sometimes comes. For I knew that someday, sometime, this *meeting* would come again with others – and it has.

LESLIE KENTON
from *All I Ever Wanted
Was a Baby*

THE LITTLE PEOPLE

A dreary place would this earth be
Were there no little people in it;
The song of life would lose its mirth,
Were there no children to begin it;

No forms, like buds to grow,
And make the admiring heart surrender;
No little hands on breast and brow,
To keep the thrilling love-chords tender.

The sterner souls would grow more stern,
Unfeeling nature more inhuman,
And man to stoic coldness turn,
And woman would be less than woman.

Life's song, indeed, would lose its charm,
Were there no babies to begin it;
A doleful place this world would be,
Were there no little people in it.

J. G. WHITTIER

GREAT INCONVENIENCE

TO KING LEOPOLD   5 January 1841

I think, dearest Uncle, you cannot really wish me to be the 'Mamma d'une *nombreuse* famille,' for I think you will see with me the great inconvenience a large family would be to us all, and particularly to the country, independent of the hardship and inconvenience to myself; men never think, at least seldom think, what a hard task it is for us women to go through this very often. God's will be done, and if He decrees that we are to have a great number of children why we must try to bring them up as useful and exemplary members of society.... I think you would be amused to see Albert dancing her in his arms; he makes a capital nurse (which I do not, and she is much too heavy for me to carry), and she already seems so happy to go to him.

The christening will be at Buckingham Palace on the 10th of February, our dear marriage-day.

QUEEN VICTORIA

TO THE PRINCESS ROYAL   2 May 1859

An ugly baby is a very nasty object – and the prettiest is frightful when undressed – till about four months; in short as long as they have their big body and little limbs and that terrible frog-like action.

QUEEN VICTORIA

BABY SONG

From the private ease of Mother's womb
I fall into the lighted room.

Why don't they simply put me back
Where it is warm and wet and black?

But one thing follows on another.
Things were different inside Mother.

Padded and jolly I would ride
The perfect comfort of her inside.

They tuck me in a rustling bed
– I lie there, raging, small, and red.

I may sleep soon, I may forget,
But I won't forget that I regret.

A rain of blood poured round her womb,
But all time roars outside this room.

THOM GUNN

My son would not have been born,
To fetch me lotus for my bosom,
To gladden my heart and my house,
Had I not smiled upon his father.
I count it a blessing that my son was born, and
That wisdom is in smiling.

ALUN LEWIS

The father darts out on the stairs
To listen to that keening
In the upper room, for a change of note
That signifies distress, to scotch disaster,
The kettle humming in the room behind.

He thinks, on tiptoe, ears-a-strain,
The cool dawn rising like the moon:
'Must not appear and pick him up;
He mustn't think he has me springing
To his beck and call,'
The kettle rattling behind the kitchen door.

He has him springing
A-quiver on the landing –
For a distress-note, a change of key,
To gallop up the stairs to him
To take him up, light as a violin,
And stroke his back until he smiles.
He sidles in the kitchen
And pours his tea....

And again stands hearkening
For milk cracking the lungs.
There's a little panting,
A cough: the thumb's in: he'll sleep,
The cup of tea cooling on the kitchen table.

Can he go in now to his chair and think
Of the miracle of breath, pick up a book,
Ready at all times to take it at a run
And intervene between him and disaster,
Sipping his cold tea as the sun comes up?

He returns to bed
And feels like something, with the door ajar,
Crouched in the bracken, alert, with big eyes
For the hunter, death, disaster.

PETER REDGROVE

from
FROST AT MIDNIGHT

Dear Babe, that sleepest cradled by my side,
Whose gentle breathings, heard in this deep calm,
Fill up the interspersed vacancies
And momentary pauses of the thought!
My babe so beautiful! it thrills my heart
With tender gladness, thus to look at thee,
And think that thou shalt learn far other lore,
And in far other scenes! For I was reared
In the great city, pent 'mid cloisters dim,
And saw nought lovely but the sky and stars.
But *thou*, my babe! shalt wander like a breeze
By lakes and sandy shores....

Therefore all seasons shall be sweet to thee,
Whether the summer clothe the general earth
With greenness, or the redbreast sit and sing
Betwixt the tufts of snow on the bare branch
Of mossy apple-tree, while the night thatch
Smokes in the sun-thaw; whether the eave-drops fall
Heard only in the trances of the blast,
Or if the secret ministry of frost
Shall hang them up in silent icicles,
Quietly shining to the quiet Moon.

SAMUEL TAYLOR COLERIDGE

Playing with Baby (detail)
CHARLES JAMES LEWIS
1830-1892

Pat-a-Cake
GEORGE ELGAR HICKS
1824-1914

I Know a Baby

I know a baby, such a baby, –
Round blue eyes and cheeks of pink,
Such an elbow furrowed with dimples,
Such a wrist where creases sink.

'Cuddle and love me, cuddle and love me,'
Crows the mouth of coral pink:
Oh the bald head, and oh the sweet lips,
And oh the sleepy eyes that wink!

CHRISTINA ROSSETTI

LAUGHTER

When the first baby laughed for the first
time the laugh broke into a thousand
pieces and they all went skipping about
and that was the beginning of the fairies.

J.M. BARRIE

A New Rival

Nothing provokes like prohibition. The baby's room is strictly out of bounds, do I make myself clear, children? But it is warm as the womb, dark at the strangest of times, and smells all new and chemisty. Moreover, it contains the mother who until such a short time ago was entirely theirs but who now spends her time in this penumbra, cradling the incomer like a bomb.

Worse, the bomb, which keeps on exploding, without any apparent damage to its own casing, looks very much as Amy and Simon did in the photos of three and four years ago. It is all too galling and the Punic missions are frequent. Here is an extract from a typical war council meeting, recorded a fortnight before the birth:

First Child (female): What shall we do when the baby comes out?

Second Child (male): I'm going to bite him's woolly off and drop him on concrete.

First Child: What if it's a gel?

Second Child: I'll still bite him's woolly off and drop him on concrete.

It was a boy and, at the time of writing, the manifesto is unfulfilled.

ALAN FRANKS,
from *Real Life with Small Children Underfoot*

PUN

We had a little baby girl
Who made our hearts to flutter.
We used to call her Margarine –
We hadn't any but her.

HERBERT R. ALLPORT

William grew, stretched, changed shape. This seemed to happen in the twinkling of an eye and with the luxurious slowness with which he himself would examine the progress of a caterpillar. The feeble hands that clutched became square, gluey exploring fingers that could pick up the smallest crumb. The jerking bowed legs became massively creased and then, used, grew to muscle. Stephanie watched his vertebrae expand. He sat on the ground and beat it with a skittle, a blue beaker. He lay grounded for weeks on his Buddha-belly and then one day was up, swaying precariously like Blake's Nebuchadnezzar on purposeful hands and untouched, soft-skinned knees. He went rapidly backwards, focusing on a coalscuttle, butting against a bookcase on the other side of the room. He stood, with wavering hands and jack-knifing knees. He walked, from skirt to chair, moving slowly round the room, clutching and puffing, raising his plump foot high and planting it. She thought she would never forget any of these moments, these points of development, these markers in time, and forgot all of them as the next stage seemed to be William and eternal....

He would sit on her knee and look at her face, testing her contours with fingers that in the early days, judging distances, jabbed at a bright eye or clawed at a lip-corner, and grew rapidly skilled at caressing, patting her cheek, tangling her hair. She saw herself in him: the learning face was her face. They looked into each other's eyes and she saw herself reflected, a looming light, a loving moon, part of himself? His flesh was her flesh, but his look was not her look....

She would hold him up, when he cried, to window or lamp, saying, 'There, Will, look at the light, look at the light.'

And very early in his life he would repeat ''igh, 'igh.' She taught him also early book, cat, flower and he applied these names extensively, using 'boo' of pictures and newspapers, 'cat' of all animals, and 'fowa' of vegetables, trees, feathers and once of his grandmother's modesty-front, poking out of the neck of her dress. He sat regally on Stephanie's knee and named farmyards and jungles of pictured beasts, cow, hoss, gog, 'en, zeb-a, effunt, 'nake, 'raffe, whale. These things are banal enough and it is hard to write the wonder with which, in a mood of distance from the everyday and the solid, a woman can hear a voice speak where there has only been a wail, a snuffle, a cry, a mutter of syllables. Will's voice was a *new* voice, speaking words that had been spoken generation after generation. Look at the light. I love you.

A.S. BYATT,
from *Still Life*

43

L'enfant Glacé

When Baby's cries grew hard to bear
I popped him in the Frigidaire.
I never would have done so if
I'd known that he'd be frozen stiff.
My wife said: 'George, I'm so unhappy!
Our darling's now completely frappé!'

HARRY GRAHAM

A TERRIBLE INFANT

I recollect a nurse called Ann,
    Who carried me about the grass,
And one fine day a fine young man
    Came up, and kissed the pretty lass.
She did not make the least objection!
    Thinks I, *'Aha!*
    When I can talk I'll tell Mamma!'
– And that's my earliest recollection.

FREDERICK LOCKER

The door opened, and Merle found herself in a long room. It was almost entirely filled with babies' cradles.

Babies' cradles of every description! Some quite grand ones, trimmed with rows of ribbon and lace, so grand that you would never have thought of giving them such a simple name as cradle, but would have at once decided that they were 'bassinettes'. Some quite ordinary basket cradles, some old-fashioned wooden ones that had evidently been used for more than one generation of babies, and some not proper cradles at all. One was an old tin bath, another a big basket, and another a wooden box....

She was most devoted to any baby; she loved the whole baby race, as every girl should do, and, in fact, as every right-minded girl does.

Well, Merle peeped into the first cradle. It happened to be one of the grandly trimmed ones. In it was lying a very small, very thin, very pale, but very clean baby. Any one who was not fond of babies would have said, 'What an ugly baby!' Merle only thought, 'That poor baby looks ill!'....

There was a ticket fastened to one of the curtains. On the ticket was written – Merle looked twice, she thought she must have made a mistake; but no, there it was plainly written, 'The Finest Baby in the World'.

She was rather astonished, for she felt sure that she had seen finer babies many a time.

In the next cradle – the tin bath one – lay a very bonnie baby, also wide-awake and perfectly happy. This was quite a different-looking baby. It had rosy cheeks and curly hair, though rather a dirty face. It really was a fine baby. Merle saw a ticket fastened to this cradle, and when she looked at it, she saw written on that too, 'The Finest Baby in the World'.

Then she looked at the next cradle, and on that was another ticket with exactly the same words on it. She looked at another, and another, and another – it was just the same all the way round – every baby, pretty or plain, clean or dirty, thin or fat, each one was labelled, 'The Finest Baby in the World'.

Merle stood bewildered. What could it all mean?

'It is simple nonsense!' she said aloud. 'There can be only one *finest* baby in the whole world.'

'That's just the point....' Standing close beside her was a small boy who looked about three years old, but who spoke as if he were very much older.

'Just it,' he repeated decidedly; 'that's just what we want to find out, which is the finest?'

Merle stared at him, amazed.... 'How is it that all these babies are labelled, 'The Finest Baby in the World?' Who gave them their labels?'

'Their mothers, of course,' said Thomas Muriel.

MAGGIE BROWNE,
from *Wanted – A King*

A VIEW FROM THE PRAM

You know, I still feel in my wrists certain echoes of the pram-pusher's knack, such as, for example, the glib downward pressure one applied to the handle in order to have the carriage tip up and climb the curb. First came an elaborate mouse-gray vehicle of Belgian make, with fat autoid tyres and luxurious springs, so large that it could not enter our puny elevator. It rolled on sidewalks in slow stately mystery, with the trapped baby inside lying supine, well covered with down, silk and fur; only his eyes moved, warily, and sometimes they turned upward with one swift sweep of their showy lashes to follow the receding of branch-patterned blueness that flowed away from the edge of the half-cocked hood of the carriage, and presently he would dart a suspicious glance at my face to see if the teasing trees and sky did not belong, perhaps, to the same order of things as did rattles and parental humour. There followed a lighter carriage, and in this, as he spun along, he would tend to rise, straining at his straps; clutching at the edges; standing there less like the groggy passenger of a pleasure boat than like an entranced scientist in a spaceship; surveying the speckled skeins of a live, warm world; eyeing with philosophic interest the pillow he had managed to throw overboard; falling out himself when a strap burst one day. Still later he rode in one of those small contraptions called strollers; from initial springy and secure heights the child came lower and lower, until, when he was about one and a half, he touched ground in front of the moving stroller by slipping forward out of his seat and beating the sidewalk with his heels in anticipation of being set loose in some public garden. A new wave of evolution started to swell, gradually lifting him again from the ground, when, for his second birthday, he received a four-foot-long, silver-painted Mercedes racing car operated by inside pedals, like an organ, and in this he used to drive with a pumping, clanking noise up and down the sidewalk....

VLADIMIR NABOKOV,
from *Speak, Memory*

BUT THE BABY SMILES SO MUCH

I remember the flash of insight I had in 1940 as I sat talking to a small delegation that had come to ask me to address a women's congress. I had my baby on my lap, and as we talked I recalled my psychology professor's explanation of why women are less productive than men. He had referred to a letter written by Harriet Beecher Stowe in which she said that she had in mind to write a novel about slavery, but the baby cried so much. It suddenly occurred to me that it would have been much more plausible if she had said 'but the baby smiles so much'. It is not that women have less impulse than men to be creative and productive. But through the ages having children, for women who wanted children, has been so satisfying that it has taken some special circumstance – spinsterhood, barrenness, or widowhood – to let women give their whole minds to other work.

MARGARET MEAD,
from *Blackberry Winter: My Earlier Years*

SOMETHING HAPPENED

I began changing when I was pregnant with Vanessa. I had been wanting that child so much, for so long. Don't forget I was 30. And something happened to me while that baby was growing inside me. I began feeling a unity with people, to understand that we do not give life to a human being to have it killed by B-52 bombs or have it jailed by Fascists or destroyed by social injustice.

I began to love people and become involved with causes.

JANE FONDA

TRUST YOURSELF

Trust yourself. You know more than you think you do.... It may surprise you to hear that the more people have studied different methods of bringing up children the more they have come to the conclusion that what good mothers and fathers instinctively feel like doing for their babies is usually best.

BENJAMIN SPOCK,
from *Baby and Child Care*

DAZZLING AFFECTION

I was continually amazed by the way in which I could watch for hours nothing but the small movements of her hands, and the fleeting expressions of her face. She was a very happy child, and once she learned to smile, she never stopped; at first she would smile at anything, at parking meters and dogs and strangers, but as she grew older she began to favour me, and nothing gave me more delight than her evident preference. I suppose I had not really expected her to dislike and resent me from birth, though I was quite prepared for resentment to follow later on, but I certainly had not anticipated such wreathing, dazzling gaiety of affection from her whenever I happened to catch her eye. Gradually I began to realize that she liked me, that she had no option to liking me, and that unless I took great pains to alienate her she would go on liking me, for a couple of years at least. It was very pleasant to receive such uncritical love, because it left me free to bestow love; my kisses were met by small warm rubbery unrejecting cheeks and soft dovey mumblings of delight.

MARGARET DRABBLE,
from *The Millstone*

On the Picture of a Sleeping Child

Sweet babe, whose image here expressed
Does thy peaceful slumbers show;
Guilt or fear, to break thy rest,
Never did thy spirits know.

Soothing slumbers, soft repose,
Such as mock the painter's skill,
Such as innocence bestows,
Harmless infant, lull thee still!

WILLIAM COWPER

A Baby's Hands

A baby's hands, like rosebuds furled
Whence yet no leaf expands,
Ope if you touch, though close upcurled,
A baby's hands.

Then, fast as warriors grip their brands
When battle's bolt is hurled,
They close, clenched hard like tightening bands.

No rosebuds yet by dawn impearled
Match, even in loveliest lands,
The sweetest flowers in all the world –
A baby's hands.

ALGERNON CHARLES SWINBURNE

No Such Flowers

The world has no such flowers in any land
And no such pearl in any gulf the sea,
As any babe on any mother's knee.

ALGERNON CHARLES SWINBURNE

Rock-a-bye Baby (detail)
HELEN ALLINGHAM
1848-1926

Baby's First Birthday (detail)
F. D. HARDY
1827-1911

MARION'S BABY

There he lay upon his back,
The yearling creature, warm and moist with life
To the bottom of his dimples – and to the ends
Of the lovely tumbled curls about his face;
For since he had been covered over-much
To keep him from the light-glare, both his cheeks
Were hot and scarlet as the first live rose
The shepherd's heart-blood ebbed away into
The faster for his love. And love was here
As instant; in the pretty baby-mouth,
Shut close as if for dreaming that it sucked,
The little naked feet, drawn up the way
Of nestled birdlings; everything so soft
And tender – to the tiny holdfast hands
Which, closing on a finger into sleep,
Had kept a mould of't.

ELIZABETH BARRETT BROWNING,
from *Aurora Leigh*

MY GIRL

As she grew and changed, I was increasingly wondering what this new girl could be, with her ecstatic adorations and rages. The beaming knife-keen awakening, cracking the dawn like an egg, her furies at the small frets of living, the long fat slumbers, almost continental in their reaches, the bedtimes of chuckles, private jokes and languors.

And who was I to her? The rough dark shadow of pummelling games and shouts, the cosy frightener, the tossing and swinging arms, lifting the body to the highest point of hysteria before lowering it back again to the safe male smell.

But she was my girl now, the second force in my life, and with her puffed, knowing eyes, forever moving with colour and light, she was well aware of it.

LAURIE LEE,
from *Two Women*

A child's a plaything for an hour;
Its pretty tricks we try
For that, or for a longer space;
Then tire, and lay it by.

But I knew one, that to itself
All seasons could control;
That would have mock'd the sense of pain
Out of a grieved soul.

Thou, straggler into loving arms,
Young climber-up of knees,
When I forget thy thousand ways
Then life and all shall cease.

MARY LAMB

The Early Years
of My Daughter Marianne

Unexpected pleasure has occasionally made her cry: seeing her Papa after an absence of a few days; and I thought tears were not a common manifestation of joy in children so young, not thirteen months old yet.... She is very *feminine* I think, in her quietness, which is as far removed from inactivity of mind as possible. She sits on the ground much more than she did, amusing herself pretty well (this amusing *herself*, has been, I fear, more my theory than my practice). I do not think she shows much perseverance, otherwise she would try longer to reach her playthings herself, etc, but this *may be* bodily inability....

She dislikes *finishing* her food and, by a curious sort of fancy, often refuses the last two or three spoonfuls through dread of coming to the bottom....

We have been puzzled for a punishment. The usual one, putting the little offender into a corner, had no effect with her, as she made it into a game to 'I *do* into a corner and be naughty little girl....'

She is very touching in her sweet little marks of affection. Once or twice, when I have seemed unhappy about little things, she has come and held up her sweet mouth to be kissed. Last night I was in pain, and made a sort of moan. She was lying by me, apparently asleep; but as if her gentle instinct of love prompted her even then, she pressed to me, saying, 'Kiss, Mama.' These are trifles, but how very precious may the remembrance of them become....

ELIZABETH GASKELL,
from *My Diary* (1835)

MY BABY

My baby has a mottled fist,
My baby has a neck in creases;
My baby kisses and is kissed,
For he's the very thing for kisses.

CHRISTINA ROSSETTI

WAR BABY

He has not even seen you, he
Who gave you your mortality;
And you, so small, how can you guess
His courage or his loveliness?

Yet in my quiet mind I pray
He passed you on the darkling way –
His death, your birth, so much the same –
And holding you, breathed once your name.

PAMELA HOLMES

A GIRL

I have a child; so fair
As golden flowers is she,
My Cleïs, all my care.
I'd not give her away
For Lydia's wide sway
Nor lands men long to see.

SAPPHO
to her daughter (600BC)

THE SALUTATION

These little limbs,
These eyes and hands which here I find,
This panting heart wherewith my Life begins;
Where have ye been? Behind
What curtain were ye from me hid so long?
Where was, in what abyss, my new-made tongue?…

When silent I
So many thousand thousand Years
Beneath the Dust did in a *Chaos* lie,
How could I *Smiles* or *Tears*,
Or *Lips*, or *Hands*, or *Eyes*, or *Ears* perceive?
Welcome ye Treasures which I now receive.

From Dust I rise
And out of Nothing now awake;
These brighter Regions which salute mine Eyes
A Gift from God I take:
The Earth, the Seas, the Light, the lofty Skies,
The Sun and Stars are mine; if these I prize.

A Stranger here
Strange things doth meet, strange Glory see,
Strange Treasures lodg'd in this fair World appear,
Strange all and New to me:
But that they *mine* should be who Nothing was,
That Strangest is of all; yet brought to pass.

THOMAS TRAHERNE

GOLDEN SLUMBERS

Golden slumbers kiss your eyes,
Smiles awake you when you rise.
Sleep, pretty wantons, do not cry,
And I will sing a lullaby:
Rock them, rock them, lullaby.

Care is heavy, therefore sleep you;
You are care, and care must keep you.
Sleep, pretty wantons, do not cry,
And I will sing a lullaby:
Rock them, rock them, lullaby.

THOMAS DEKKER

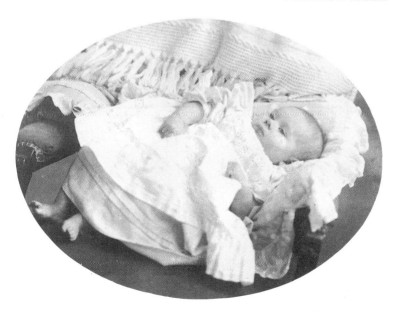

A Father's Lullaby

'Lullaby, oh, lullaby!'
Thus I heard a father cry,
'Lullaby, oh, lullaby!
That brat will never shut an eye;
Hither come, some power divine!
Close his lids or open mine!

'Lullaby, oh, lullaby!'
What the devil makes him cry?
Lullaby, oh, lullaby!
Still he stares – I wonder why?
Why are not the sons of earth
Blind, like puppies, from the birth?

'Lullaby, oh, lullaby!'
Thus I heard the father cry;
'Lullaby, oh, Lullaby!
Mary, you must come and try! –
Hush, oh, hush, for mercy's sake –
The more I sing, the more you wake!

'Lullaby, oh, lullaby!
Two such nights, and I shall die!
Lullaby, oh, lullaby!
He'll be bruised, and so shall I, –
How can I from bedposts keep,
When I'm walking in my sleep?'

THOMAS HOOD

Teething Problems

It was a peculiarity of this baby to be always cutting teeth. Whether they never came, or whether they came and went away again, is not in evidence; but it had certainly cut enough, on the showing of Mrs Tetterby, to make a handsome dental provision for the sign of the Bull and Mouth.... Mrs Tetterby always said, 'it was coming through, and then the child would be herself'; and still it never did come through, and the child continued to be somebody else.

Charles Dickens,
from *The Haunted Man*

Brahms' Lullaby

Lullaby and goodnight
With lilies of white,
And roses of red
To pillow your head:
May you wake when the day
Chases darkness away,
May you wake when the day
Chases darkness away.

Lullaby and goodnight
Let angels of light,
Spread wings round your bed
And guard you from dread.
Slumber gently and deep
In the dreamland of sleep,
Slumber gently and deep
In the dreamland of sleep.

JOHANNES BRAHMS

A Cradle Song

Sleep, Sleep, beauty bright
Dreaming o'er the joys of night.
Sleep, Sleep; in thy sleep
Little sorrows sit & weep.

Sweet Babe, in thy face
Soft desires I can trace,
Secret joys & secret smiles,
Little pretty infant wiles.

As thy softest limbs I feel,
Smiles as of the morning steal
O'er thy cheek, & o'er thy breast
Where thy little heart does rest.

O, the cunning wiles that creep
In thy little heart asleep.
When thy little heart does wake,
Then the dreadful lightnings break,

From thy cheek & from thy eye,
O'er the youthful harvests nigh.
Infant wiles & infant smiles
Heaven & Earth of peace beguiles.

WILLIAM BLAKE

TO MY DAUGHTER

Bright clasp of her whole hand round my finger,
My daughter, as we walk together now.
All my life I'll feel a ring invisibly
Circle this bone with shining: when she is grown
Far from today as her eyes are far already.

STEPHEN SPENDER

HYMN OF JOY

Children in the wind – hair floating, tossing, a
miniature of the agitated Trees, below which they play'd –
the elder whirling for joy, the other in petticoats, a fat Baby,
eddying half willingly, half by force of the Gust – driven
backward, struggling forward – both drunk with the
pleasure, both shouting their hymn of Joy.

SAMUEL TAYLOR COLERIDGE,
from his *Notebooks* (1797)

FOR GEORGINA

Laughing little buttercup
    Sunbeam of the meadows
Ear of wheat among the corn
    Fledgling of the hedgerows

Mimic of the open air
    Seeking the way the wind went
Stern to escape, swift to return
    Fearlessly dependent

May you ever hide and skip
    By Cherwell or by Granta
Innocent as you are now
    My golden-haired enchanter.

FRANCIS WARNER

ACKNOWLEDGEMENTS

The editor and publisher gratefully acknowledge permission to reproduce copyright material in this book:

Lauren Bacall: from *By Myself*, by kind permission of the author and Jonathan Cape; Johannes Brahms: 'Cradle Song' translated by Iris Rogers from *Classical Songs for Children* by Marian Harewood and Ronald Duncan, reprinted by permission of Anthony Blond; A S Byatt: from *Still Life* by permission of the author and Chatto & Windus; Walter de la Mare: 'The Birthnight' by permission of The Literary Trustees of Walter de la Mare and The Society of Authors as their representative; Margaret Drabble: from *The Millstone* by permission of the author and Weidenfeld & Nicolson, also 'With All My Love, (Signed)Mama' copyright The New York Times Company (*New York Times*); Isadora Duncan: from *My Life*. Copyright 1927 by Boni & Liveright. Copyright renewed 1955 by Liveright Publishing Corporation. Reprinted by permission; Jane Fonda: from an article in *Woman's Own*, reprinted by permission of Jane Kesner Ardmore; Alan Franks: from *Real Life with Small Children Underfoot* by permission of the author and J M Dent; Harry Graham: 'L'Enfant Glacé' from *More Ruthless Rhymes for Heartless Homes* by permission of Edward Arnold Ltd; Thomas Gunn: 'Baby Song' from *Jack Straw's Castle* by permission of the author and Faber & Faber; Pamela Holmes: 'War Baby' from *The Sunday Times* by permission of the author; Langston Hughes: 'Birth' from *Fields of Wonder* by permission of Alfred A Knopf; Leslie Kenton: from an article 'All I ever wanted was a baby', reprinted by permission of the author; Philip Larkin: 'Born Yesterday' from *The Less Deceived*, reprinted by permission of The Marvell Press, England; Laurie Lee: from *Two Women* by permission of the author and Andre Deutsch Ltd; Alun Lewis: 'The Merchant's Wife' from *Raider's Dawn* by permission of the author and George Allen & Unwin Ltd; Margaret Mead: from *Blackberry Winter* by permission of the author and Angus & Robertson; Vladimir Nabokov: from *Speak, Memory* by permission of Vera Nabokov; Sylvia Plath: 'Morning Song' from *Ariel* published by Faber & Faber, London. Reprinted by permission of Ted Hughes; Peter Redgrove: 'Early Morning Feed' from *The Collector and other Poems* by permission of the author and Routledge & Kegan Paul; Carl Sandburg: 'Being Born is Important' from *Complete Poems* by Carl Sandburg by permission of Harcourt Brace Jovanovich Inc; Sappho: 'A Girl' translated by C M Bowra, from *The Oxford Book of Greek Verse in Translation* edited by T F Higham and C M Bowra (1938) by permission of The Oxford University Press: Stephen Spender: 'To My Daughter' from *Collected Poems* by Stephen Spender by permission of Faber & Faber; Benjamin Spock: from *Baby and Child Care* by permission of the author and The Bodley Head; Francis Warner: 'To Georgina' from *The Collected Poems* by permission of the author and Colin Smythe.

Paintings

Lady Laura Alma-Tadema's 'A Mother and Child' by kind permission of the Hahn Gallery; Fred W Ewell's 'The Firstborn' (detail of) by kind permission of the Ferens Art Gallery, City of Kingston Upon Hull; F D Hardy's 'Baby's First Birthday' (detail of) by kind permission of Wolverhampton Art Gallery and Museums; George Elgar Hicks's 'Pat-a-Cake' by kind permission of Dr and Mrs Kenneth Watson; Charles James Lewis's 'Playing With Baby' (detail of) by kind permission of the Christopher Wood Gallery; John Phillip's 'A Scottish Christening' (detail of) by kind permission of Christie's, London; William Strutt's 'Beneath an Angel's Wing' by kind permission of the Christopher Wood Gallery.